START-UP
HISTORY

◄ • • • • • • • • • • • • • • • • • • ►

Homes

Stewart Ross

W
FRANKLIN WATTS
LONDON • SYDNEY

First published in 2014 by Franklin Watts

Franklin Watts
338 Euston Road
London NW1 3BH

Franklin Watts Australia
Level 17/207 Kent Street
Sydney, NSW 2000

Produced for Franklin Watts by
White-Thomson Publishing Ltd

www.wtpub.co.uk
+44 (0) 843 208 7460

Editor: Anna Lee
Consultant: Nora Granger
Designer: Tessa Barwick

This book was first published by Evans Brothers Ltd.
It has been revised and fully updated in line with the KS1
history curriculum.

A CIP catalogue record for this book is available from the
British Library.

Dewey no: 643'.09
Hardback ISBN: 978 1 4451 3502 1
Library eBook ISBN: 978 1 4451 3503 8

Printed in China

Franklin Watts is a division of Hachette Children's Books,
an Hachette UK company.
www.hachette.co.uk

Picture Acknowledgements: Beamish The Living
Museum of the North: 19r; Bridgeman 21; Chris Dorney/
Shutterstock: 4t; Chris Fairclough: 5r, 6b, 7b; Shutterstock:
4b, 6t, 7t, 15r, 16-17dps, 20; Thinkstock: cover t, cover
b; York Museums Trust (York Castle Museum): 8-9dps,
10, 11t, 11b, 12-13dps, 14, 15l, 18, 19l, cover main; Zul
Mukhida: 5l

Contents

Different houses

▼ **This is a bungalow.**
It was built about 20 years ago.

▲ **This is a
block of flats.
It is about
40 years old.**

bungalow   built   years   ago   flats

▼ **This house was built about 90 years ago.**

▲ **This terraced house is more than 110 years old. It is Victorian.**

old   terraced   house   Victorian

Roofs and windows

◀ **Here is the roof of the bungalow. It has clay tiles.**

▶ **The roof of the terraced house has slate tiles. It has many chimneys.**

6
..... roof clay tiles slate chimneys

◀ **The bungalow has plastic window frames.**

▶ **The terraced house has sash windows. The frames are made of wood. How do they open?**

plastic window frames sash wood 7

Inside a Victorian house

This is a living room from Victorian times.

The **mantelpiece** is over the **fireplace**. ········

What can you see on the mantelpiece?

mantelpiece   fireplace   pictures

There are many pictures on the walls.

The floor is covered with a rug. Underneath the rug are floorboards.

How is this living room different from your living room at home?

rug   floorboards   home

Fireplaces

Here is the Victorian fireplace.

The coal scuttle and tongs are next to the fire.

What are the tongs for?

coal scuttle   tongs

▲ This fire is in a house that is 60 years old. It uses electricity.

▶ This modern fire uses gas. but looks as if it burns wood.

electricity   modern   gas   burns

A kitchen from the past

This is a kitchen from about 70 years ago.

How is the sink different from the sink in your kitchen?

kitchen   sink

There is a **pressure cooker** on the **stove**.

The **kettle** is also on the stove.
Most modern kitchens have electric kettles.

How else is this kitchen different from a modern one?

pressure cooker   **stove**   **kettle**   **13**

Changing cookers

This Victorian cooker was called a 'range'.

It burned wood or coal.

Food cooked slowly in the oven beside the fire. . . . . . .

cooker   range   coal

▼ This is an electric cooker from 60 years ago.

How is it the same as a modern cooker?
How is it different?

▲ This modern microwave uses electricity.
It cooks food very quickly.

oven   microwave

A modern bathroom

▶ **This** bathroom has a basin, a bath and a toilet.

What else can you see that belongs in a bathroom?

bathroom   basin   bath   toilet

◀ **There is a shower over the bath.**

In the past, many homes didn't have bathrooms.

People washed in a tin bathtub in the kitchen or the living room.

shower past tin bathtub **17**

Toilets inside and outside

Here is the toilet in a modern bathroom.

The seat and lid are made from plastic.

seat   lid   flushed

◀ **This toilet is from about 70 years ago.**
It was flushed by pulling the handle on the end of the chain.

▲ **One hundred years ago most toilets were like this one.**
They were found outside the house.

handle   chain   outside

Which is older?

One of these bedrooms is modern and one is Victorian. Can you tell which is which?

Look carefully at the beds, the furniture and the decoration.

bedrooms   beds

The bedroom on the left is modern.
The one on the right is from Victorian times.

furniture   decoration   **21**

New history and homes words highlighted in the text:

ago	clay	gas	oven	slate
basin	coal	handle	past	stove
bath	coal scuttle	home	pictures	terraced
bathroom	cooker	house	plastic	tiles
bathtub	decoration	kettle	pressure cooker	tin
bedrooms	electricity	kitchen	range	toilet
beds	fireplace	lid	roof	tongs
built	flats	mantelpiece	rug	Victorian
bungalow	floorboards	microwave	sash	window
burns	flushed	modern	seat	wood
chain	frames	old	shower	years
chimneys	furniture	outside	sink	

Background Information

CHRONOLOGY OF SELECTED BACKGROUND INFORMATION

1890s Electric light in homes of the well-off.
Bulk of the population living in sub-standard housing without gas, electricity, bathroom or inside lavatory.

1900 First electric cookers appearing. Gas cookers widespread in wealthy homes.

1907 First electric washing machine.

1919-24 Increased subsidies for council housing.

1919-39 2.5 million private homes built. Average price of a 'semi' £450.

1935 12% of the population living in overcrowded conditions (two or more per room).

1936 17.8% of the population of York unable to afford adequate food, housing, heating and lighting.

1939 90% of homes heated by open fires. 66% homes wired for electricity.

1947 Green belts introduced around large cities.

1948 Microwave oven invented.

1951 33% of British homes without a plumbed bath.

1954 Transistor radios available.

1956 22.5% of Scottish homes overcrowded.

1960s St Anne's district of Nottingham: 91% of homes with outside lavatory; 85% without bathrooms, 54% without a hot water system.

Parents and Teachers

1970s   Fitted carpets and use of showers (rather than baths) becoming widespread.

1980s   Home ownership growing rapidly.

1990s   Housing shortage owing to swiftly growing number of households.

2000s   Houses become greener with doorstep recycling collection, solar panels and triple glazing.

2008   Worldwide credit crunch damages housing market.

2010s   Multigenerational homes become common again as house prices increase.

2013   Over 90% of households have internet access.

Possible Activities:

Visit to nearby homes of different periods.

Draw features of homes from different periods.

Make a frieze timeline.

Work out how people lived from the objects that surrounded them – e.g. the amount of time needed to clean a range meant that it either stayed dirty or someone spent a long time each week cleaning it. Who?

Make a 'home corner' of different rooms and periods.

Invite adults in to talk about their homes at some specific time in the past.

Some Topics for Discussion:

Differences between homes of the same period – e.g. Victorian mansion and slum.

Role of servants before labour-saving devices.

Health and the spread of bathrooms and flushing toilets.

Safety in the home – open fires, etc.

Changing design and materials for household objects.

Further Information

BOOKS

FOR CHILDREN

Houses Long Ago (See Inside) by Rob Lloyd Jones and Barry Ablett (Usborne, 2010)

Project Geography: Homes by Sally Hewitt (Franklin Watts, 2013)

Where You Live: Houses and Homes by Ruth Nason (Franklin Watts, 2010)

Your Local Area: Homes by Ruth Thomson (Wayland, 2012)

FOR ADULTS

At Home: A Short History of Private Life by Bill Bryson (Black Swan, 2011)

If Walls Could Talk: An Intimate History of the Home by Lucy Worsley (Faber & Faber, 2012)

The Great Indoors: At Home in the Modern British House by Ben Highmore (Profile Books, 2014)

WEBSITES

www.bbc.co.uk/scotland/education/wwww/homes/kids/index_choice.shtml

www.geffrye-museum.org.uk/kidszone

history.parkfieldict.co.uk/modern1950s/1950s-homes

www.primaryhomeworkhelp.co.uk/houses.html

PLACES TO VISIT

The Geffrye Museum, London

Victoria and Albert Museum, London

York Castle Museum

Index

24